DINOSAUR DINNERS

SHAARON COSNER

D1214033

A FIRST BOOK
FRANKLIN WATTS
New York / London / Toronto / Sydney / 1991

Photographs courtesy of: American Museum of Natural History: pp. 12, 13, 16, 17, 19, 20, 22, 23, 27, 32, 35, 36, 40, 42, 46, 47; Animals Animals/Earth Scenes: pp. 24, 28 (both Breck P. Kent), 33 (E.R. Degginger), 43 (Mickey Gibson), 51 bottom (Walter Fendrich); New York Public Library, Picture Collection: pp. 25, 26, 29, 31, 41, 43 insert; Photo Researchers Inc.: pp. 37 (Dr. Jeremy Burgess), 50 top, 51 top (both Gregory Dimijian), 50 bottom (M. Philip Kahl, Jr.; USDA/Forest Service: p. 49.

Library of Congress Cataloging-in-Publication Data

Cosner, Shaaron.
Dinosaur dinners / by Shaaron Cosner.
p.   cm.—(A First book)
Includes bibliographical references and index.
Summary: Examines the eating habits of a variety of dinosaurs as well as their ability to adapt to their environment.
ISBN 0-531-20011-6
1. Dinosaurs—Food—Juvenile literature.   [1. Dinosaurs.]
I. Title.   II. Series.
QE862.D5C729   1991
567.9'1—dc20
90-47225   CIP   AC

To Brett, alias "Littlefoot"

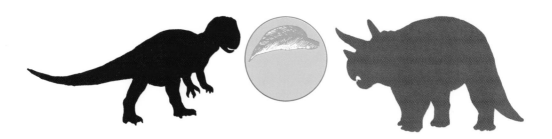

CONTENTS

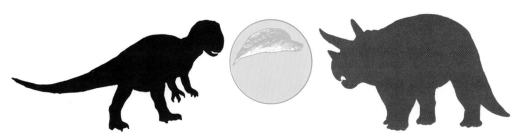

DINOSAUR
DINNERS

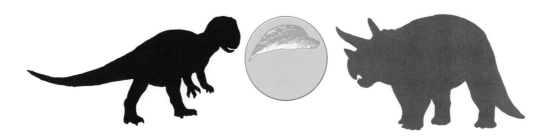

INTRODUCTION

Every animal on earth must eat. Every animal must change food into energy in order to live. The smallest insect must eat. The biggest elephant must eat.

But what about the huge, 85-ton (about 86,000-kg) dinosaurs that were as big as seventeen elephants? They didn't have zoo feeders to feed them. They didn't have fast-food restaurants. And, since some of the biggest dinosaurs probably ate a half ton of food in one day, where did they find enough food to fill those huge bodies? And what did they eat?

Dinosaurs could live together in the same area as long as they were not dependent on the same sources—or each other—for food. In this painting, allosaurus, stegosaurus, and others are shown at the water's edge.

PLANT-EATING DINOSAURS

One way scientists can tell what the dinosaurs might have eaten is by looking at fossils. Fossils are pieces of plants or animals that have been preserved in rock. Their living tissues were replaced with minerals dissolved in water. Scientists have found fossils of dinosaur teeth, bones, footprints, and skin impressions.

Some fossils show that an animal had food in its stomach when it died. The shape of a tooth fossil also helps the scientists tell what kind of food the dinosaurs ate. The fossils of plant leaves, pollen, and stems or trunks tell the scientists which plants might have been living at the same time as the dinosaurs.

The texture of a dinosaur's hide can be seen in this piece of fossilized dinosaur skin. This fossil helps us to picture what a dinosaur actually looked like, something that bones alone cannot do.

These people are sitting in fossils of footprints made by dinosaurs. By studying these footprints, scientists can tell a great deal about dinosaurs' structure, weight, and speed.

Some plants that the dinosaurs ate were probably very tough. The bigger plant-eaters must have had to eat a lot of plants before they were full. They would need big, strong stomachs to hold all that food. Their teeth and jaws would also have to be strong enough to cut and grind tough plants into pieces small enough to digest.

One of the biggest chompers of all time was anatosaurus. Anatosaurus didn't care how tough a plant was. This dinosaur had many rows of teeth along the sides of its mouth. Anatosaurus could have hundreds of teeth in its mouth at any one time!

Not all plant-eaters had many teeth, strong stomachs, or big bodies. Anchisaurus, for instance, had a long neck, so it could reach high into the trees. And its teeth were sharp enough to chew tasty leaves.

One of the biggest plant-eaters was stegosaurus. It had a huge tail with spikes at the end, which it used for protection. It also had bony plates standing upright on its back. Scientists think these plates may have helped to regulate the body temperature of stegosaurus. Its strong back muscles might have made it possible for the huge body to be supported by the hind legs. But since stegosaurus's front feet were not adapted for anything ex-

The large stomach of this dinosaur held the large amount of food it needed in order to stay alive. Its long neck enabled it to eat from the tops of trees that some other dinosaurs could not reach.

A fossilized anatosaurus is on display here, protected in a glass case. It's often difficult for visitors to picture this mass of bones as an animal that lived and breathed. Even scientists have had trouble putting dinosaur bones back together. Some fossilized bones were put together incorrectly, but with further research the mistakes were discovered and corrected.

cept walking, this was probably not the case. It is more likely that stegosaurus stayed on all fours, feeding on low ground vegetation that was easy for its low-positioned head to reach.

But like anatosaurus, stegosaurus probably ate only soft leaves. Despite its huge body, its teeth were small and weak. Even so, if you weigh hundreds of pounds, you could probably munch up a lot of plants in one day!

Brachiosaurus didn't have a strong tail to help it stand, but if you weigh 70 tons (about 71,000 kg), that might not help anyway. It had a long neck that reached about 28 feet (about 9 m), and it could reach 40 feet high (about 12 m) into the trees.

It took a lot of food to keep a 70-ton brachiosaurus full. This eager diner probably ate all day long. Some days it might have eaten 500 to 1,000 pounds (about 227 to 454 kg) of vegetation, but if you looked at its teeth you would wonder how it could manage that. Its teeth were like small pegs.

For one thing, some scientists believe brachiosaurus had a nostril on top of its head. This might have enabled it to eat without stopping to breathe.

Another thing brachiosaurus might have had was a special kind of stomach called a gizzard. (Birds also have gizzards.) When the food went down into the gizzard, the gizzard squeezed and

The plates on stegosaurus's back were supplied with blood. The sun warmed the blood in these plates, and the blood then traveled throughout the animal, warming it.

The plates on stegosaurus's back really gave it one of the first solar-powered heating systems!

Brachiosaurus's front legs were longer than its back legs, which probably helped it reach into trees. Note the nostril on top of its head—this may have developed so that breathing would not interfere with eating.

squashed the food against hard things such as pebbles or pieces of dirt that had gotten mixed up with the plants. These small stones were called gastroliths. In addition to its teeth, gastroliths in brachiosaurus's gizzard helped grind down the plant food.

Not all dinosaurs were tall enough to reach leaves in tall trees. Some were low feeders—plant-eaters that ate food that grew close to the ground.

*Triceratops is a bit like animals we know today.
It looks a great deal like a rhinoceros. Although
triceratops used its horns mainly for defense,
the males locked horns and wrestled with other
males, much as modern deer and antelope do.*

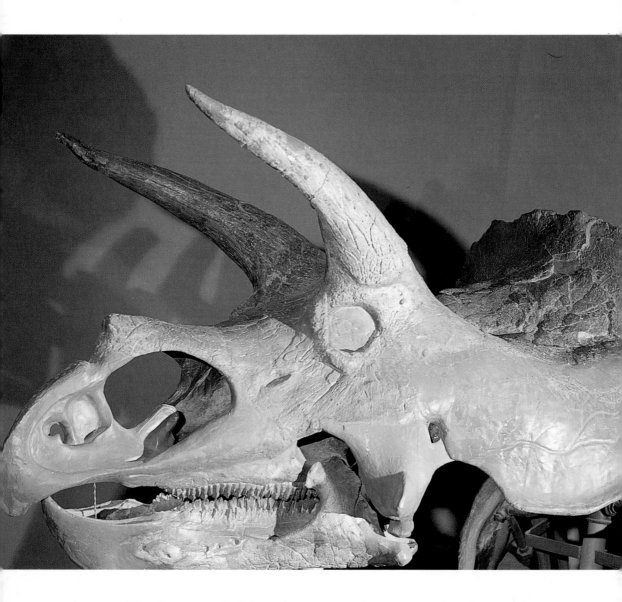

The horns of this triceratops have survived time and the elements, and are still sharp and pointed.

Because the horn on
parasaurolophus's head
was hollow, scientists
now think it was a type of
sound vibrator through which
the dinosaur could hoot.

One example is the 6-to-9-ton (6,200- to-9,000-kg) triceratops. It had a beak like a turtle, which it used to eat plants near the ground.

Another low-plant eater was parasaurolophus. This dinosaur had a mouth that looked like a duck's bill. It had strong teeth that could grind up even the toughest plants.

THE PLANTS
THEY ATE

What types of plants were found on the menu of a plant-eating dinosaur? One of the oldest kinds of plants on earth are algae. There is fossil evidence that algae lived millions of years ago at the same time as dinosaurs. Different types of algae range in size from one-celled microscopic forms to kelp, which can grow to 30 feet (9 m). Today, algae is a food source for animals and human beings. It was probably also used as a food source by plant-eating dinosaurs.

Many of the plants the dinosaurs ate looked very much like plants and trees we know today. Some plant fossils have been found that look like horsetails and ferns growing today in wetlands or swamps.

31

Fossils of algae prove that they lived when the dinosaurs did and could have been a source of food.

*Not all algae are small; this giant kelp
would be quite a meal for any animal.*

Some looked like trees we see all around us. Pine trees and cypress trees look like trees that the dinosaurs ate. So do palm trees.

Some of the leaves the dinosaurs ate looked like pine needles. The narrow, spiky leaves of some ferns also look just like some of the leaves dinosaurs ate.

Some of the plants that grew at the same time as dinosaurs had flowers on them. Scientists have found fossils of flowers in the United States, Italy, and England. These flowering plants had a single stem with many flowers on short branches.

Scientists think these plants (called cycads), stored food for a long time. Then they burst into bloom all at once. After that they died. When they burst into bloom, they could have several hundred flowers on one stem. In fact, one fossil found in the Black Hills of South Dakota had between five hundred and six hundred flowers.

With so many giant plant-eaters around, it might seem that all the plants would soon be eaten up. But plants were protected in ways that helped them to survive. Some grew thorns and spines. Some grew fibers so tough that no dinosaur would want to eat them.

Bee-like insects also appeared at this time. Eighty-five percent of flowering plants depend on

Above and next page: these fossils of pinecones and a plant leaf (over) are clues to what types of plants lived at the same time as dinosaurs. Note the resemblance between the fossils and similar plants we see today.

See the pollen that has collected on this honeybee as it searches for nectar in flowers. Insects such as bees may have helped the dinosaurs survive by helping flowering plants reproduce—just as bees help flowering plants reproduce today.

insect pollination for reproduction. Bees spend most of their time flying from flower to flower looking for food. As a bee searches for the pollen and nectar in a flower, some pollen falls onto its body from the anther of the flower. The pollen on the bee's body brushes off on the stigma of the flower, or onto the stigma of another flower the bee goes to in its quest for food. Pollen must be transferred from the anther to the stigma in order for flowering plants to reproduce. The appearance of bees during the dinosaurs' time helped ensure the reproduction of flowering plants, a food source of plant-eating dinosaurs.

MEAT-EATING DINOSAURS

Not all dinosaurs were plant-eaters (called herbivores). Some ate meat. These meat-eaters (called carnivores) had special adaptations that helped them get their food. They didn't have to be big or have large stomachs, because they didn't have to eat as much as the plant-eaters. If you've ever eaten a salad, you know it doesn't fill you up as much as a steak!

The meat-eaters had to have good eyes and noses to help them find other animals to eat. They had to be fast to catch their prey. And they had to have fairly large brains to outsmart their prey.

Meat-eating dinosaurs also had to have very sharp teeth and claws. Deinonychus, for example, had a deadly curved toe claw. (Deinonychus is Greek for "terrible claw.") Because it was usually

39

*This allosaurus skull shows the
large brain cavity and sharp teeth
needed by carnivorous dinosaurs.*

This large iguanodon (right) is being attacked by a group of fierce, meat-eating deinonychuses.

*Above: allosaurus, a famous meat-eater, finishes
a meal of an apatosaurus.
Right: the very short arms of tyrannosaurus rex
make this model at the Calgary Zoo
an easily recognized figure.*

only 3 to 5 feet (.9 to 1.5 m) tall and weighed 150 to 175 pounds (about 68 to 79 kg), it might have run with others in a pack. They tracked and overcame plant-eaters such as tenontosaurus, which weighed 2 tons (about 1,814 kg) and stood at 20 feet (about 6 m). One deinonychus would never be able to beat the tenontosaurus in a fight. But in a pack, deinonychuses could probably surround the helpless plant-eater and slash it with their claws until it died. Then they could eat it.

Deinonychus had teeth with edges that looked like a steak knife. It also had a large muscle under its throat. This muscle made the throat expand so that large chunks of meat could go down easily. A huge jaw allowed it to open its mouth very wide for those big chunks.

Another fierce meat-eater was allosaurus. Allosaurus had large, powerful jaws and strong legs with claws. It probably used the claws to hold its prey down while it ate.

One of the most familiar dinosaurs, tyrannosaurus rex, was also a meat-eater. In fact, it has been called the king of the meat-eaters. Its huge jaws were 4 feet (about 1.2 m) long. Inside its mouth were approximately sixty teeth. Each tooth was from 3 to 6 inches (7.5 to 15 cm) long. These teeth made it easy for tyrannosaurus rex to kill and tear apart its food.

THE BATTLE
FOR SURVIVAL

For over 150 million years, plant-eating and meat-eating dinosaurs lived on earth. Then dinosaurs died out. How did they become extinct?

Some people think dinosaurs died because the earth changed. During most of the period when the dinosaurs lived, the earth was very warm. There were swamps with lots of plants living in the green, misty waters. Then, slowly, the continents moved. Large pieces of earth rose from the waters and many of the warm seas disappeared. The world was also getting colder.

Scientists had once classified dinosaurs as reptiles, and thought they were cold-blooded. This would mean they needed to absorb the heat around them. But in recent years, some scientists have de-

There are many different
theories on why the dinosaurs
vanished. One theory holds
that the climate changed
and the warm, swampy areas
disappeared, taking with them
many of the plants that
these herbivores ate.

cided that dinosaurs might have been warm-blooded. Some had upright postures, high food intake, and microscopic bone structure like mammals, which are warm-blooded.

Perhaps some dinosaurs were warm-blooded and some were cold-blooded. Those that could not tolerate the cold would lose their energy and become very sluggish as the world started getting colder. This might have made it easier for those that could stand the cold to eat those that could not.

The cold also brought about new trees. Trees that survived in cold weather lost their leaves in the winter. And those plants that could not survive the cold weather died in the winter. Thus some scientists believe that for many months, the plant-eating dinosaurs didn't have anything to eat.

Other scientists believe that death for the dinosaurs came from space. Perhaps a comet or shower of comets struck the earth. Perhaps an asteroid or a very large meteorite struck the earth. Dust from an asteroid or meteorite could block out light and heat from the sun for months or years. The plants would die, and then so would the plant-eaters.

When the plant-eaters died because of a lack of

*Many trees survive cold winters but
lose their leaves. As trees like
these maples evolved, the dinosaurs
had less to eat during the winter.*

Snakes, crocodiles, lizards, and turtles are the
modern descendants of the dinosaurs. There is a
resemblance between these animals of the past
and the present: note the similarities between the
crocodile's mouth (above) and those of some
dinosaurs. The collard lizard (top right) also looks
like some of the extinct giants of
the earth, only much smaller.

food, this meant that there was less food for the meat-eaters. Then they, too, became extinct.

The smaller reptiles like the crocodiles, lizards, snakes, and turtles did not die. And all the plants did not die. It was the great giants of the earth— the dinosaurs—who ran out of food. We are still finding out about dinosaurs and why dinnertime, for them, was over.

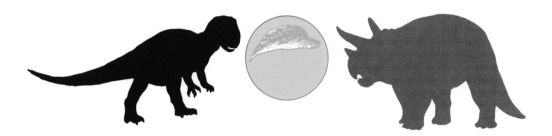

GLOSSARY

Algae—plants that do not have roots, stems, flowers, or leaves.

Allosaurus—a dinosaur that walked on two legs and balanced itself with its tail. It was about 16 feet (about 5 m) tall when it stood on its hind legs.

Anatosaurus—a duck-billed dinosaur. Anatosaurus lived in North America and possibly England and was one of the last of the duck-bills to become extinct.

Anchisaurus—one of the first dinosaurs to be discovered in North America (1818). It had narrow feet and a small head. It was about 8 feet (about 2.5 m) long.

Asteroids—minor planets with orbits that lie mostly between Mars and Jupiter.

Biped—an animal walking on two feet, like human beings.

Brachiosaurus—one of the largest known land dinosaurs. Many were taller than a four-story building and weighed 70 to 85 tons (about 71,000 to 86,000 kg), seventeen times heavier than the biggest elephant today. It had a long neck that reached about 28 feet (about 8.5 m) high.

Comet—a body in our solar system made out of ice and dust that orbits the sun in an elliptical pattern.

Deinonychus—a fast bipedal dinosaur with large claws on its feet and hands. Fossils of this dinosaur have been found in Montana.

Extinct—coming to an end; no longer existing.

Fossils—pieces of once-living organisms that have been preserved in stone.

Gastroliths—stony masses in the stomach.

Gizzard—a muscular area that grinds food before it goes to the stomach; found in some birds.

Meteorite—a mass of stone or metal that falls to earth from outer space.

Parasaurolophus—a duck-billed dinosaur with a hollow tube that extended over its shoulders. It might have had webbed hands and a duck-bill shaped like a spoon.

Stegosaurus—a dinosaur covered with bony plates of armor. Stegosaurus was about 25 feet (about 8 m) long, and had a very small head and brain.

Tenontosaurus—a huge dinosaur that weighed 2 tons (about 2,200 kg) or more.

Triceratops—one of the last horned dinosaurs to develop and one of the last to become extinct. It had a smooth, solid frill around its neck and three horns on top of its head.

Tyrannosaurus rex—a dinosaur known for its great size, sharp teeth, and claws. It was almost 50 feet (about 15 m) from its jaws to its tail.

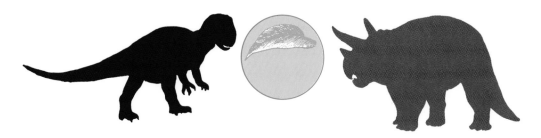

FOR
FURTHER
READING

Aliki. *Digging Up Dinosaurs*. New York: Harper & Row, 1988.

Cobb, Vicki. *The Monsters Who Died: A Mystery About Dinosaurs*. New York: Putnam, 1983.

Lambert, David. *Dinosaurs*. New York: Franklin Watts, 1990.

Lampton, Christopher. *Mass Extinctions*. New York: Franklin Watts, 1986.

Lauber, Patricia. *Dinosaurs Walked Here*. New York: Bradbury Press, 1987.

Norman, David, and Angela Milner. *Dinosaur*. New York: Alfred A. Knopf, 1989.

INDEX

ABOUT
THE AUTHOR

Shaaron Cosner is the author of nine nonfiction books for children. She teaches English to sophomores and seniors at Corona del Sol High School. She lives with her husband in Tempe, Arizona, and is the mother of two and grandmother of four.